MW00737983

Let's Just Take This

OUTSIDE!

*"A humorous look at the people and situations
that cause frustration in the workplace."*

by Ty Brown

— Katsir Publishing —

"Let's Just Take This Outside! *A humorous look at the people and situations that cause frustration in the workplace."*
Copyright © 2003, by Ty Brown. Printed and bound in the United States of America. All rights reserved. No part of this book may be reproduced or transmitted in any form or by any means, electronic or mechanical, including photocopying, recording or by an information storage and retrieval system without permission in writing from Katsir Publishing.

ISBN: 0-9722705-0-7
Library of Congress Control Number: 2002093488

Published by:
Katsir Publishing
39270 Paseo Padre Parkway #256
Fremont, CA 94538-1616

Visit our website at www.katsirpublishing.com for additional information.

Copy Editor, Christine Taylor, ctaylor533@earthlink.net
Cover and illustrations, Kevin Duffy, www.kevinduffy.net
Book design and layout, Foglia Publications, rsf@foglia.com

To my family and friends...

<u>Acknowledgements</u>

I would like to thank everyone that encouraged me to write this book.

To my wonderful husband Nadav, I love you and thank you for your insight, support, and encouragement. You gave me reassurance, hugs, and kisses during many of the tough moments that led to this book.

Thank you Kevin Duffy for your flexibility and your wonderful illustrations that capture the real humor in what we take too seriously.

Thank you Christine Taylor and Rochelle Ware for coming in at just the right time and making much needed corrections. You really took a load off of me. I am happy that you love to read.

Finally, thanks to all of you that are now reading "Let's Just Take This Outside!" I appreciate your curiosity and your sense of humor.

Table of Contents

Preface

No matter how strongly I support the right of others to have their opinions on any and all matters, I still have moments of lucidity that bombard me with two important facts:

1. There is really only one right answer for most questions, and

2. There is only one good resolution for most conflicts.

Therefore, I find it utterly ridiculous that seemingly intelligent adults can't agree on even the simplest matters.

During my stretch in corporate America, I spent many hours in useless meetings designed to do nothing more than give the appearance of intelligent leadership, logical thinking, and detailed planning. So many times I played in my head the most intelligent words anyone could have said at those moments: "Work with me people! This is a no brainer! It's not rocket science!"... and so on, and so on.

As if the two or three hours spent in those futile summits were not enough, each resulted in a long list of action items that served only to waste more time. Had it not been for the even more frustrating events that commonly occurred during each workday, I would have avoided these meetings like a hornets' nest. But many times they were the only refuge available.

As frustrating as the meetings were, the petty personal conflicts that arose between these same adults were even more exasperating. At any moment, two otherwise rational people, raised on different principles, in different cultures, with different goals, could become engaged in a battle over differences that seemed trivial. With all of the things they could have legitimately argued about, they choose things as simple as titles, entitlement, more office space, less office space, 8 am versus 9 am meetings, Friday versus Monday deadlines, and other easy problems. Many times I wondered if I was in a professional office with adults or a high school gym with teenagers.

Rather than talking things out face to face, they waged email wars. They spread rumors faster than a wildfire could consume a dry Arizona forest. The psychological and emotional damage they created could make the physical destruction from hurricane Hugo look like the aftermath of a tailgate party. With all of their education, they still hadn't learned that a difference of opinion is almost a guarantee when there are two brains in the room. And unless you want to play the role of the vegetable, you had better learn to accept it.

Yes, it was everything they didn't teach me about corporate America and I didn't know to ask. It seems that everyone, Mom, Dad, my six sisters, two brothers, college professors, mentors, and even my best friends forgot to mention that although success was not impossible, I had to first figure out how to get around the other human beings in my way. That, at times, seemed impossible.

All I wanted was a soapbox to let it all out. To yell. To scream. To stomp. I am sure that it would have relieved my frustration. But I learned early on that soapboxes, unlike the other events of the workday, were considered to be unprofessional and a waste of time. Actually, it wasn't so much the soapbox as the emotional dramatics required for an effective execution.

With so much building up inside and soapboxes not an option, I had to find other ways to express myself. Most common was my immediate trans-formation into a clinched jawed, fast paced, swift moving production machine. The phrases: "I want no part of this, I just wasn't raised that way, it's against my religion to take part in these petty office conflicts," became convenient weapons. As long as I kept moving, I could escape. Everything and anything needed to be done and got done. Rapid pounding of my fingers on the computer keyboard, deadly silence, and strong body language, which screamed, *"YES, I AM ANGRY! YES, I AM TOO BUSY! YES, STAY AWAY FROM ME! BE AFRAID, BE VERY AFRAID!"* guarded me like a steel barrier. What can I say? It was a temporary solution and it worked— for me.

I didn't always run away from it all. I tried. I reeeally, reeeally tried. I presented countless hours of intelligent, logical, and passionate arguments. Still, I could not pierce the barricade of ignorance. Human nature preceded my efforts by millions of years. So, no matter how clearly I presented my case, no matter how much evidence supported my argument, and despite the fact everyone had previously agreed and supported this resolution, this was another day and the right to express an opposing opinion would take precedence even if it made no darn sense. So deal with it! The useless meetings continued. The petty conflicts went unresolved. And the vicious backbiting escalated daily.

These situations aroused in me a state of good ole' backyard anger that only a trip to the backyard (where fists could be thrown and bodies could roll) could pacify. So I say now what I could not say then:

"Let's Just Take This Outside!"

Warm Up

LIFE–small word, big meaning; a tasteful substitute for the expletive meaning, "screwed," when the unexplained, undeserved, unexpected have occurred and you are unprepared. Just living can induce these inopportune moments. Waking up, growing up, sharing things, sharing experiences, buying things, making friends and losing friends, all at any moment may present some form of "screwed." But in retrospect, none of them can match what I endured while working in corporate America.

I suppose that most of my opinions on these LIFE experiences are framed by my perception of what the words "corporate America" represent. I am of the opinion that using these two words together has provided an impenetrable shelter for stereotypes, racism, envy, jealousy, and even revenge. All of which most working Americans have fallen victim to at some point in their lives. It can be extremely frustrating to the point of feeling that the only solution is to "take it outside" and physically fight it out. When all else fails, everybody loves a good fight!

You understand.

Anyway, I was talking about the words "corporate America." When I hear them, my mind builds pictures of tall buildings, large offices, big desks, computers and expensive suits. No bodies. No faces. Just a huge glass structure where things just…happen.

What do you see?

I actually prefer to use the term "workplace." Immediately the glass shatters. Walls fall down. Human beings emerge. There are people moving around, working in large offices, using computers and wearing those nice suits. Executives, managers, co-workers, white, black, tall, short, fat, thin, friendly, phony...people. Living, thinking, feeling human beings that must accept responsibility for all of the joy and all of the pain of LIFE.

Today with so many people claiming to be victims during the aftermath of their poor decisions, this may appear to be about someone to blame. It's not. However, it is about recognizing that we victimize ourselves by falling for the "corporate America" explanation. It is about recognizing that we, working human beings, have built this glass structure that shields us from the responsibility of the decisions we make in the workplace, the decisions that affect the lives of other human beings. No, it's absolutely not about blame. It's about accountability.

Still Warming Up...

Beware of the sarcasm used here lest you should also begin to find your workplace unbearable. My words may appear to be bitter. Yes, another human carcass left behind as road kill by the "corporate bus." I am of the opinion that this is more likely to be the attitude of those of you that have had the privilege of doing most of the driving.

My mission in this warm up is to let you know that while you were driving like a bat out of hell, taking all the wrong turns, I, as well as others, swayed dangerously. On a bench seat. Without the required seatbelts to secure my docile butt to the bench! Only now do I realize that my contentment with this arrangement was in anticipation of my opportunity to show off my driving skills. I was never told that I had the right to expect a pleasant, safe and secure ride no matter what seat I occupied. Instead, as my body swayed ferociously, I held on for dear life. I pacified myself with mental images of your sincere smiles and firm handshakes. I hummed to the sound of your voice during your quarterly speeches: "Our people are our biggest assets." "Trust me." "Everyone here is important." "We work daily to secure your futures and not put you and the company at risk." Ahhh, the soothing words of bus drivers everywhere. Oh, and lest I should appear ungrateful, thanks for the ride.

Today there seems to be an onslaught of these well-dressed charlatans running companies right into the ground. If I wasn't already tired of these idiots ruining lives because of what appeared to be *"legitimate"* poor decisions, I would certainly be fed up with their most recent cons. They have apparently outsmarted everyone once again. They aren't even trying to camouflage their cons anymore. Forget cajoling and deception, go straight to the money. There are so many ways to steal it. Borrow three hundred million or more. What about a little insider trading? You know the company is about to bottom out. Don't tell the employees or the investors. This is your chance to get the gold. Hurry now, off to the ski cottage and just...think...Yes. Think about what's best for the company. That's it!

If it weren't so criminal, it would actually be kind of funny.

I guess it's only fair that I dedicate a little time to the newest dot com executives. They are not in the aforementioned category for two reasons, they don't have the experience and they are certainly not well dressed. Besides, their problem is more about walking around with their heads up their butts. Really, how much power do you think you have? How arrogant can you allow yourself to be? You are basically leading a group of volunteers. Ok, some magazine quoted your comments on next generation fiber optic products. You now have more than 15 minutes of fame. Come down to earth will ya! If this thing doesn't pan out, you will be one of us again and that same magazine will be lining somebody's birdcage. Relax! Chill out! It's not as if you're Bill Gates or John Chambers...yet.

If *it* weren't ridiculous, *it* would be funny.

Finally, the Introduction

Unlike other books by better writers, I won't offer any quick solutions to your workplace woes. Not directly anyway. My goal is simply to share my observations, my assessments, my pain. Maybe just knowing that you are not alone will make it easier for you to get through each workday. Not to mention that I finally have my soapbox.

At some point you may be able to relate to the victim (this has happened to you) as you read. You have my deepest empathy. But, I implore you to challenge your self-awareness and compare yourself to the villain (have you done this to anyone). If you find a common characteristic or two and come to the realization that you have been the oppressor in any workplace conflict, make a conscious decision to never do it again. If you will do that, then indirectly, we have offered a solution that may put an end to all of our workplace woes. If you can't abstain from your villainous ways, then I encourage you and others like you to telecommute as often as possible.

Throughout the book, I overuse the phrase, "I am of the opinion..." I use it because I am very opinionated. It helps me emphasize that fact. I tried other phrases like "I think," "I suspect," "I believe," and a few more. But, they all seemed to weaken the point that this is my valid, substantiated, expert opinion and over emphasized the fact that this is *JUST* my entitled opinion. I am of the opinion (there I go again) that if one is going to write a book, then one must find a way to convince the reader that a few valid, substantiated opinions stated matter-offactly, are at the time stated, actual facts. Only then can the author convince you, in spite of your better judgment, that he or she is credible and therefore gain your allegiance.

But seriously, I sincerely believe that there are some valuable lessons that can be learned from each of the situations presented here. Try not to view them as just criticisms because they do paint vivid pictures of actual workplace conflicts. They also highlight some of the pitfalls to avoid in the workplace. Therefore, at the end of each chapter, which I call "Rounds," I conclude with a "Workplace Improvement Principle" (WIP). Each principle could be the "moral," if you will, of each story. I am of the opinion that the person that practices these principles will be a better person, a better employee, and will rarely cause frustration in their workplace.

So, hang in there and enjoy reading it.

Let's Get

Ready to

Rumblllle!

ROUND 1

Tick Tock, Is It Five O'Clock?

A new job is the open door to new opportunities. This is your big chance to make valuable contributions. Gain new experiences. Learn from past mistakes and most of all **STAY AWAKE.**

May I introduce the problem?

I am of the opinion that after six to eight months on most jobs, the professional challenge is over and the biggest daily challenge becomes maintaining the appearance of interest while fighting the weight of your eyelids. They feel like a mere 3 lbs at your desk. Not a problem, light aerobics is good for facial muscles. Look young, feel young. Then the weight increases to 5 lbs during general conversations with your co-workers. A bit more challenging but not impossible. A little black coffee and you're as good as new. But the jump to 10 lbs during any and all meetings is just too darn much. I am sorry, but I don't think there is one human being alive that can keep their eyelids open with 10 lbs of weight sitting on them. The weight puuuulls your entire head sloooowly, sloooowly down until your chin is resting juuuuust above your chest aaaand…SNAP! You caught it just in time. Ohhhh, but there it goes again…aaaand SNAP! Another save. Pretty soon you realize that you either sprain your neck or simply rest your head on the conference table. If you position your forehead on your hands, you can pretend to have a headache. I recommend that you try hard to avoid the deepest possible sleep. You must be prepared to respond when your name is called. And it will be called. Don't worry, just answer with "Ahhh, let me think about it. I'll take it as an action item and get back to you." It works every time. Even if the answer doesn't fit the question, it still works. You just camouflaged sleep as distraction and everyone sympathizes with that. Oops, I stated that the biggest professional challenge was over. But, if you consider falling asleep at work to be unprofessional, then you still have that one professional challenge.

* * * * * * * * * * * * * * * * * * * *

John worked the third shift for a large manufacturing company. He monitored one of the stations on the assembly line. He admitted that the job was not very difficult just boring. So, once he got things rolling along on the line, he could basically do whatever he wanted. At least, this was the way he felt about it.

John's manager became suspicious of the third shift employees because the production numbers were consistently lower than the other shifts. He was especially concerned about John's station because his numbers were always the lowest. See, the third shift worked autonomously because the manager's day ended when the third shift began. So after checking them in, he went home. The manager felt that they were doing more goofing off than working because he was not there to watch them. He decided to investigate.

The manager began by making a few calls to John's station from his home. No one answered. One day he spoke with John about it and he stated that he must have gone on break, to the restroom or to another station. Each time there was a legitimate reason. The manager accepted them and warned

John that his station should not be unattended. If he took a break, he was to ask someone to watch things until he returned.

One night the manager decided to come to the plant and check up on John. He looked everywhere, starting with his station. John was not there. He went to the lunch area, he was not there either. Finally, he decided to check the men's room. There John was, asleep on one of the benches in the locker area.

The manager decided not to wake him. This was his chance to finally get rid of this unproductive guy. He ran to his office and got a camera. He took pictures of John sleeping. John had no idea. An hour later he came back. John was still asleep. He took another picture. He went to John's station and worked until the shift was over. When he saw John returning, he left. He didn't want to be seen.

The next night, John reported to work and the manager pretended to go home. An hour later, he returned to check on John. He was not at his station. The manager went directly to the locker room and there was John, asleep again. This time the manager took pictures in two-hour intervals. Each time John was fast asleep. He returned to John's station and worked the production line once again and waited. At the end of the shift, John returned to turn off the machines. And once again the manager ducked out so that John would not see him.

The manager repeated this for the third consecutive night and John repeated his evening shift of sleep. But this time when John returned to his station, the manager was there waiting.

He told John to meet him in his office. John knew he was in trouble but he had a production line of lies ready to save his job.

As John began to explain how he just didn't feel well that evening and took a short nap, the manager displayed the pictures of him sleeping the two previous nights. As he began to express his right to take breaks and sleep on his lunch hour, the manager displayed an array of pictures taken in one and two hour increments for three days. He could not lie his way out of this one. He was caught. And he was fired!

When I asked the manager why he had allowed John to do this for three days he explained that John was a very skillful liar and would convince most people that he had done nothing wrong. He had worked there for many years and had become adept at fooling everyone. Plus, he was really a nice guy. He further explained that John was a member of an organization that had a lot of influence at their facility. If he didn't have solid proof, John would never have been fired and would be right back at work the next day. So he wanted to make sure he covered all of the bases.

⁕ ⁕ ⁕ ⁕ ⁕ ⁕ ⁕ ⁕ ⁕ ⁕ ⁕ ⁕ ⁕ ⁕ ⁕ ⁕ ⁕ ⁕ ⁕ ⁕

John presents an extreme case. Sure, he may have been bored, but I say he was mostly lazy. He had no integrity. He had no self-respect. He chose to get paid for work he didn't do. But just because John worked in a manufacturing environment doesn't make him a special case. I have walked by cubicles and offices and seen more screen savers with heads bobbing up and down in front of them than I can count. These people are in the same category as

John. Not because they napped once, but because this was their daily routine. The only thing unique about John's situation is that he actually found a comfortable place to lie down.

There are some jobs that I would consider to be an exception to the boredom rule. They would be those that are constantly presenting opportunities for new projects, incomplete projects or at least 50% travel. But I am of the opinion that rarely do we call these "jobs." We usually give these the affectionate term, "careers." Notice the soft, melodious tone of the vowels in this word versus the harsh sounding consonants in "jobs." Clearly this is an indication, maybe even a warning, of what is to be expected from either.

When I find myself in a job situation left with only the professional challenge of staying awake, hey, I go get another job! For some, this may seem rather extreme. For others, it may seem logical. The rest of us just see it as survival. It's not rocket science. We don't need to analyze it. We have to work. We want to work. We want to succeed. We don't want to be bored out of our minds!

So, for the first few months, I am blessed with the delusions and pleasures of a new career. I am happy. I come to work singing. I sing while I work. And I leave work singing. But when my song fades because the job monster has reared its ugly head, I must find new opportunities that support the delusions that make me happy. I must repeat the career process. If you are going to try this, hang in there for at least one year. Experience has taught me that this makes it easier to start over.

You: "Corporate America calls this job hopping."

Me: "Well, yes they do. And yes it is."

You: "It is really frowned upon."

Me: "Yes. So what? Hey, family, fun and having a life are also frowned upon in corporate America. So whose standards are you going to trust?"

The corporate/company rules change constantly. It all depends on what the company is promoting. Keep this in mind when deciding who knows what is best for you. Also keep in mind that these are the same people who quickly reminded you, and actually taught you, that change was good. To stay flexible. Think out of the box. Yeah, right! I say JUMP out of the darn box–their box. Because as soon as the company needs to move you to a different department/job, that is exactly what is going to happen. They want to decide when you will be allowed to move around. They attach their five-year plan to most positions for this purpose. As I stated, it is all about what is convenient for the system. By the way, your job-hopping usually is NOT. So when they begin to allow us to take their jobs and turn them into careers, we won't have to hop around.

* * * * * * * * * * * * * * * * * * * *

Workplace Improvement Principle

WIP #1

Put your heart and soul into your work.
If that becomes your biggest daily challenge,
find other work.

ROUND 2

Old Horses Still Grazing

Repetitive tasks day in and day out are a leading cause of what I call a "Disengaged, Unproductive Employee" (DUE, doo-ee). I am of the opinion that these are the folks that never come out of the "job" state. Heck, I don't even think they make the distinction between job and career. They live for the paycheck and I really don't have a problem with that. I too enjoy getting that regular paycheck. My problem is only that I refuse to sacrifice the alacrity of my mind and body for anything, even the paycheck. Well, I can probably put up with any job for a period of six to nine months if I desperately need a paycheck and this job provides one. A regular one. A big one.

Let me take this opportunity to say to the animal rights people and the plain ole' horse lovers that I really like horses. I am not in any way disparaging them. Horses are known to be very hardworking animals. However, I felt that the title was appropriate because I learned that as horses age, their bodily functions are less efficient. Also, their teeth wear down. As a result, they cannot graze properly and require more attention and assistance for something as simple as eating. It immediately reminded me of a DUE.

Although this round is not about age but rather inefficiency, there is a strong analogy that can be made. Here we have someone or something once known for hard work and expected to work, suddenly becoming a burden. Inefficient. Inefficiency brought on by repetitive use, not so much overuse. True, they are still working, or like the horses, still grazing, but neither is doing a very good job of it.

Essentially, DUE's allow themselves to become dulled in the monotony of the job. They become the monotony. They wear the back and forth back and forth back and forth rhythm like a uniform. They put it on at 9 and take if off at 5. Soon, they can repeat the entire workday without entertaining one new thought. One different thought. Or even a different gesture. They can't recall the beginning, the end, or anything in between. I guess the DUE has too much professionalism to find a good place to take a nap as John did (See Round 1).

Well, in defense of monotony, or even better, repetition, I say that we are all vulnerable to the DUE disease. We all get so used to routines that they no longer require our full attention. And guess what? We don't give it!

Ok. So, you think that you're exempt. Let's see if you are...

Did you drive to and from work today? Did you drive your kids to daycare? Did you drive to the grocery store? Did you drive to any other familiar place? Ok. When you got there, could you recall the entire drive? Honestly, could you? If it was a place you drove to everyday, I doubt it. In the blink of an eye. After a few conversations on your cell phone. After a few arguments with NPR (National Public Radio). After a few good laughs with Tom Joyner, Steve Harvey, or another favorite morning show host. You were there. Let me add that you can probably recall everything *EXCEPT* the drive. Yikes! It is just by the grace of God that we don't have more fatalities while driving. Anyway, I have just proven that you are therefore *NOT* exempt from "DUEitis" because that is exactly what happens when you become used to any routine.

In manufacturing environments, the assembly lines require a lot of repetitive motion. This repetitiveness can cause problems in the body after awhile. Fortunately, most of these physical symptoms are easily detected. Some part of the body begins to ache in the joints or muscles most frequently used. Immediately you realize that these symptoms must be treated or you will eventually have a DUE.

Let's shift to my workplace, an office environment. Typing is as physical as we get. Once we get past Carpal Tunnel Syndrome and the blank stares here and there, we have no other physical warnings of repetitiveness or simple monotony. In this case, we have to look for other types of symptoms to indicate that a person is probably too used to a routine. They are too robotic in the execution of their duties. We have found that the following symptoms are pretty good indicators of a DUE or a DUE in the making:

1. Rejection of any new ideas especially those that would require more work for them

2. Defensiveness toward constructive criticism that may improve their job

3. The expectation that their seniority equals value.

And the most common symptom:

4. Overuse of the fallback argument "this is the way we have always done it," emphasizing

their reluctance to change.

• •

Doris started with Company A when she was only 19 years old. She began as a mail clerk and worked her way up amidst many obstacles. After 33 years of hard work, she is now a production supervisor and still very loyal to the company. However, Doris has one very big problem, the boulder on her shoulder.

Doris believes that she has not been treated fairly. She began to complain after the onslaught of young college "poopy pants" (as Doris called them) were hired into the company at high wages and "cushy" jobs. She thought that they should have to work their way up the way she did. She didn't see education as such a big advantage, especially when most of them had to call on her regularly for the most basic information. Yet, these young people were coming in at senior positions. This made Doris, and others of similar history, very angry.

As a result, Doris began to criticize any and every idea at every meeting. If one of the young "poopy pants" had even a notion that they were going to make any changes, she shot it down with vivid examples of previous failures using "that very same idea." This became a regular routine for Doris and everyone was rather tired of it. They tried having meetings without her, but somehow she would mysteriously appear. Her co-workers longed for ways to shut her up or get rid of her. But Doris was somewhat of a company icon.

One day, the CEO decided that it was time to reward the employees with 20 or more years of service with a special gift. He wanted each department executive to find ways to reward their 20+'ers individually so that each gift would be unique. They were to ask for ideas without revealing the purpose.

Doris's department manager called a meeting of his supervisors and asked specifically "what would be a great reward for someone that has done great service for the company for many years?" Many great ideas came up, such as, vacation plans, jewelry, stock certificates, gift certificates, and even cash. All of which were acceptable because the CEO had simply allotted a budget to each department and they were to use it at their discretion.

The final suggestion came from Doris. She stated that she was aware of a company policy that was already in place that rewarded people after 10,15, 20, 25 years and so on. This policy rewarded these groups by allowing them to select gifts from the company catalog. This policy was acceptable, had worked for years, and should be enough. She further explained that she did not think "any individual should receive special gifts for doing their job. Everyone is paid to do their job and that should be enough. The company could eventually go bankrupt if they allowed managers to reward their favorite people with company funds."

Doris had no idea what was going on. She assumed that someone ELSE was about to receive yet another undeserved reward. No one had worked harder than she had, so no one deserved anything special. She had never been recognized before and certainly this was yet another one of those times.

After her suggestion, Doris's manager had a meeting with the CEO and explained what Doris had stated.

He further expressed some concern that if they were to try to continue setting aside special funds for this every year, it could prove to be rather expensive. Together they reviewed the company's gift catalog and agreed that the gifts were adequate. The CEO cancelled the special gift idea and told his assistant to send a memo regarding this decision to all managers.

A few days later, as Doris rode home in her carpool with two other women from the company, they began their daily gripe session of the events at work. One of the young women stated that once again the company had cancelled a great idea by deciding against the special gift for those with 20+ years of service. "What special gift?" Doris asked. The young lady began to explain how she had learned from her dear friend, the assistant to the CEO, about the memo sent to all managers that the old policy of selecting gifts from the catalog would be sufficient and that the $12,000/department would not be allocated for special gifts. She further explained how someone had encouraged the managers to stick with the catalog to save the company money. It was also revealed that this conscientious individual emphasized that everyone was paid to do their job and should not be rewarded beyond the paycheck. Everyone should be thankful for the gift catalog. They had no idea that the fastidious Doris had been the culprit.

Doris could hardly swallow after she heard this story. She barely spoke for the rest of the drive home. When she got home, she flopped into one of her kitchen chairs and began to sob. During the drive home she realized what she had done. She had become so conditioned to refuting every good idea that she stopped thinking. She had become hardened and bitter.

She began to think of all the things she could have done with a special gift of cash. But in the familiar Doris fashion, her anger slowly returned and once again she acknowledged that the system was truly designed to keep her from getting what she deserved.

* *

We have all seen these symptoms because we have all worked with these unyielding "sticks in the mud," the DUE's. We have watched these DUE's shut us down in meetings. We have listened to their constant complaints in spite of *THEIR* cushy situations. And we have sat back and watched them single handedly keep the company in the dark ages.

In order to appear impartial in this situation, I should point out that Doris was once a very productive employee. She worked her way up to a supervisory position. But somewhere along the way, her focus shifted from her goals and her work, to others and their work. This is really one of the biggest problems when people become bored, dulled, or dissatisfied in their jobs.

There is not a canned solution to problems like this. I continue to hope that all DUE's will at least experience what Doris did and slam the door on themselves for a change. However, on an individual level, I have pledged that should I ever become burdened with a DUE under my leadership, I am obliged to put the company out of its misery.

* *

WIP #2

There are three ingredients that guarantee success and productivity in the workplace: **ATTENTION, ATTENTION, ATTENTION.**

1. *Pay* **ATTENTION** *to your work. Stay alert. Check the details. Go for quality first not quantity.*

2. *Pay* **ATTENTION** *to your environment. Be supportive. Be flexible. Notice when things are changing. Change with them if necessary.*

And most importantly:

3. *Pay close* **ATTENTION** *to yourself. What kind of person are you? Are you reliable? Do you do as you promised? Are you responsive? Do you do what you are asked? Are you building up or tearing down? There is no middle road on this one.*

(By the way, personal hygiene could also be included in this area. No details necessary.)

"Sound Familiar?"

ROUND 3

A Side Note On Good Paper

Your many college degrees only give you an expertise in whatever theoretical concepts you may have learned in college. Expertise in common sense is still best earned through experience, your life lessons.

While gaining this advanced theoretical knowledge, there are some complimentary lessons in life that could serve to simultaneously enhance the common sense sector of the brain. But most people tend to prefer, and therefore overuse, the abstract ideas. They get much pleasure from the feeling of superiority gained from observing the blank stares of friends previously in-sync with their views. They become so enamored with the new concepts that they tend to apply them when common sense would be a better fit. Therefore, the common sense sector of the brain goes on ice until they get over themselves or at least recognize that the rest of the world couldn't care less about their advanced college learning. Then, the best that can be expected is spurts of enlightenment during their thawing out period.

I am of the opinion that becoming an expert in the common sense category will always trail several years behind the theoretical expertise. Don't become alarmed by this observation. It is probably new information for you. As a matter of fact, the higher your level of formal education, the newer this information will appear.

What is the point? Common sense can't be

substituted for formal education and formal education can't be substituted for common sense. The two really should compliment each other. However, if I had to choose, common sense would win hands down. There are numerous examples of successful individuals without formal education, but none without common sense.

I am of the opinion that if the last use of your common sense was during the college application process, then the college degree you hold is simply a waste of good paper.

• • • • • • • • • • • • • • • • • • • •

When Larry started his new job, the company had not yet ordered a new computer for him. His manager knew he was coming a month prior to his arrival but did not bother to prepare for him. Therefore, Larry had to be placed in a temporary office away from the rest of his group. Only the manager knew that he had arrived to start his new job.

During Larry's first week, the manager had to travel on business. The following week he took his two weeks vacation. All the while Larry still had not met his co-workers.

At the beginning of the third week on his new job, Larry decided that he would find his co-workers and introduce himself. Everyone was surprised to hear that he had already been there for two weeks. They had been waiting for his arrival and assumed it would be when the manager returned from his vacation.

They chatted for a bit. Larry told them about his

many years of experience and they shared theirs. They all seemed to hit it off. Finally, after a bit more chit chat about previous jobs and what Larry would be expected to do in this new job, he asked if anyone knew when he would be getting a computer. Everyone gasped, once again shocked. Not only had he been there two full weeks, but he had been sitting at a desk without a computer. When asked what he had been doing for two weeks, his answer was, "reading."

Well, one of his co-workers picked up the phone and called the IT (Information Technology) Department and asked them to bring a loaner computer to Larry. The IT manager said that his new computer had arrived a week earlier but no one knew him or where he was sitting.

I am not sure that this is a testament to Larry not using his common sense or more to just how crafty and lazy he was. He could have tried to find his team the first week; the first day. Then he would have gotten the assistance he needed. Even with his many years of experience he had not developed enough assertiveness to get the basic requirements to do his job. Instead, he seemed to have mastered the art of waiting on things to come to him.

Maybe the person that hired him and was responsible for preparing for him is the point to this story. Well, either way you look at it. It seems neither of them used much common sense.

* *

WIP #3

Don't rest on what you know. Use what you know. Give it everything you've got, then rest.

Or maybe you prefer the older adage: "It's not what you know, but how you use it."

"I know that's not you, right?"

ROUND 4

The Grace Period

I am of the opinion that every new thing we buy, sell, trade or DO, is given a period of time in which we anticipate a revelation of the true character of this new thing. I call this the grace period.

An understanding of the grace period concept is very important on a new job. You have your grace period and the employers have theirs. Let me walk you through a successful grace period in a new job. You have impressed them enough to get an offer and they have impressed you enough to accept. Grace period begins...

If the first impression is the lasting impression, in the workplace, first impressions are made every day during the grace period. Because no matter how much you impressed them yesterday, today it is forgotten.

I know that you think you should spend the first two or three months with your nose to the grind-stone. Earning your keep. Hitting the ground running. All of the things they told you they would expect and all of the things you are ready to give.

Stop! Don't!

There is really no need to spend much time understanding your specific responsibilities. You won't be judged on how well you do your job or how quickly you learn the tasks during the grace period. This is where you will need your common sense to help you get through a little lesson in life. The most important factor during this time will be your social skills. How well do you play on THE TEAM?

Forget all of your degrees. They don't entitle you to the right to walk into a new job and feel that you have a good grasp of how to do the job. They have provided you with a level of confidence that may eventually help you trampoline to the top of the ladder, but first you must acknowledge the code of conduct that must be followed in the workplace. A part of that code explicitly states that anyone not walking around lost and confused during the first two weeks of work is a "know-it-all" and thinks he/ she is better than everyone else. Therefore, beware of the confidence level you display during those first two weeks. Have respect for "THE GRACE PERIOD."

Ok, I know I promised not to give any advice, but here it is in layman terms...

1. When Bob, Mary, Jack and several others throughout each day come over to offer assistance with all of the things you figured out years ago, act as if you are learning it for the first time. When you are instructed on how to turn on the computer, don't remind anyone that you just graduated with a degree in computer science. Fumble around for the power switch. Squeal with delight when it actually powers up. If you hear beeps and chimes during the process, well, then one more squeal won't hurt.

2. No matter how small the workplace, ask for directions to the restroom at least twice. This is a good one to use when your intelligence is so obvious you couldn't hide it if you tried. Plus, you find it difficult to be humble. This really works well with the administrative

support staff. They feel empowered.

3. Displaying a little clumsiness and disorientation a few days a week will keep your co-workers from feeling inadequate and could possibly save your job during the grace period. You are just too much for people when you are good at everything.

4. Always have an ace, something that is not quite up to par, that you can give them once in awhile. When you talk about your ineptness in this particular category, always follow with compliments on how much better they are. Remember, superstars are only acceptable in Hollywood.

These unwritten and unspoken rules must be followed to remain EFFECTIVE. To maintain order and to get the support you need to do your job. They always worked well for me. People always seemed to like me a lot better when I pretended to know absolutely nothing. I could always be one of the "gang" or "guys" in a stupidity role.

Whatever works right? After all, the goal is not dignity, self-respect, or advancement, but rather to last long enough to pay all those bills you accumulated trying to build a corporate image. Hey, believe me, there is nothing worse than being "blackballed" in an office environment (See Round 12, Now Entering Gang Territory) and intelligence seems to be the number one trait of most people on the "black list."

I am of the opinion that these people feel they have earned the right to watch you, the new guy, fumble around and make a fool of yourself the first few weeks. After all, they did it and they weren't really trying. Basically, they have earned the right to teach you all of the little things, heck everything.

The smile they give you each day is their way of complimenting themselves on how well you have turned out after their training. You are a protégé. So, when you deny them these rights, you are then denied the right to become one of them, which is your life's dream. You won't make it through the grace period.

＊ ＊ ＊ ＊ ＊ ＊ ＊ ＊ ＊ ＊ ＊ ＊ ＊ ＊ ＊ ＊ ＊ ＊ ＊

When Tim started his new job, he quickly became known as the great team player. He ran to help the other engineers. He made himself available for any support the Sales or Marketing teams needed. Everyone was very pleased with the way he was fitting in.

After a couple of weeks on the job, the VP of Sales asked Tim to join him and another member of the Sales team at a customer meeting in Dallas. The meeting went so well that Tim also went with them to two other meetings in Kansas City. When Tim returned to work the following Monday, he decided to write a trip report. He had always done this on his previous job so he was familiar with what details to include. Tim's report included everything from each of the meetings. He mentioned the customers' requests for new product features, the customers' complaints about the already installed equipment and even the lack of responses to customers' calls. He included EVERYTHING. He then emailed his detailed report to the Sales organization and copied Marketing, Engineering and the Executive Staff. He was confident that his detailed report would be greatly appreciated.

Within 10 minutes after hitting the "send" button, a war of words started. Angry emails were sent between Sales and Tim. They told him he had no right to reveal any details of their meetings. That was their job. Tim mentioned that he had heard via the other organizations that the Sales team never produced trip reports so he thought he was doing them a favor. Next, Engineering fired back at Sales because many of the features being requested were going to throw off the entire product roadmap for the next year. Plus, they had no idea that there were problems with the systems already installed. Then the CEO got involved. He wanted to know why the Sales team was not responding to these key customers. He told the VP of Sales that they were paid to be in the customers' faces everyday if necessary and that was what he wanted. The fingers kept pointing and Tim was right in the middle of it all.

Whew! Poor Tim, the great team player. The helpful applications engineer was suddenly a troublemaker. All he wanted to do was to show that he enjoyed being in the meetings and that he listened INTENTLY. What he got instead was no more invitations to any customer meetings. No one on the Sales team wanted him anywhere near their customers. He was badmouthed every time they needed an excuse for failing to produce a purchase order. Tim went from team player to scapegoat with one email.

As you may suspect, the Engineering team, the Marketing team and all of the executives were very happy with Tim's email. They were glad to finally get a trip report from a customer meeting. They were glad to know what the customers had to say about the products. However, since Tim was hired to support Sales and he was no longer welcomed, he could no longer be effective. None of the other organizations went to bat for Tim. He was ousted. So, Tim, not willing to sit around and twiddle his thumbs or surf the Internet, left the company for a better job.

• •

The people with the most confidence and assertiveness are often the ones most willing to help. They also seem to help others feel good about themselves and about their work. This should be admired. They always compliment the insecure or shy guy. They say "thank you" when someone provides assistance of any kind. They reciprocate by providing assistance when they can. They run to reward those that do their jobs well. They take a few co-workers out to lunch. They buy flowers for Secretary's Week. But no one remembers or cares about any of these things if you are otherwise "too much" during the grace period. Your confidence and assertiveness is annoying, not helpful. The grace period is your chance to be humble. To encourage them to look past your excellence and toward your false modesty. If you blow it, they won't remember any of the wonderful things about you.

You: "That sounds crazy!"

Me: "Good! That means you've never experienced it. Or have you?"

You: "I'm sure I haven't. Maybe you are just too cynical."

Me: *"Maybe?* I am definitely cynical. I just hope that you are NOT still below the expert level in the common sense category. Meaning, you have not yet figured out why you continue to get the cold shoulder and sideways glances from all of those wonderful people that were so nice to you during the job interview. You know, the ones that encouraged you to take the job. In either case, you are probably going to pay closer attention now. That's all I ask."

We are bombarded with advice on how to impress people in our new jobs. No one ever teaches us how to NOT be so impressive. Believe it or not, this is just as important and sometimes more important, especially if you plan to have a career within the walls of corporate America. But I ask myself: after all of this, why do we still want to?

* *

WIP #4

A new workplace environment can be very intimidating...remember?

Allow and expect new employees to show their strengths immediately. Encourage their assertiveness. When they make a mistake, see it as an opportunity to teach, not terrorize.

ROUND 5

What's Behind An Open Door?

I always enjoy the way upper management begins each employee orientation with the "open door policy" invitation: "If you have a problem with your manager, feel free to speak with his or her manager about it or you can come to me. I will hear you. Everyone is important here. You can expect complete confidentiality and assurance that the problem will be addressed…"

What they forget to tell you is that although everyone is important, there are degrees of importance. Most of the people have probably been there longer, have had more time to build an allegiance, and are probably MORE important. With all of their violations of company policy and all of their bad habits, they have gained SENIORITY. You on the other hand–bright eyed, protecting the company's money, revealing every weakness with your efficiency, and not yet trusted–have not.

So, immediately after your confidential meeting, prompted by your recollection of the "open door policy" speech, your boss is called in and informed of your BETRAYAL. Because most senior managers and executives are too gutless to simply state the problem, the confrontation will begin with the fact that you brought this to their attention. Something like: "I never thought this was a problem, but if this new kid is recognizing it, see if you can improve. Basically, I am very pleased with your work here so this is not a big deal…*blah blah blah.*"

In most cases these are things that they wanted to

say for months but never had the brass balls. Oops! I mean courage. You became a scapegoat and a backstabber all in one meeting. So, what we have here is a broken rung on your success ladder–a hole in the center of your trampoline. But most importantly, a lesson in loyalty: *For Members Only!* Hey, these are the same people that will "blackball" you because you have no apparent faults. Did you actually think that they would accept your criticism?

Don't misunderstand my intentions. I feel your pain! I hear your roar! Yes, there is a proper gestation period, the grace period, for everything. Get to know things before you try to change things. I clearly understand your confusion. You thought that a blatant disregard or violation of company policies was unacceptable. You thought that the CEO/leader of said company would want to know of any such violations. You thought that upper management could be trusted and that they had earned their positions by demonstrating such trust. I know! I read the same books you read while my common sense was on ice.

* *

Thelma decided to apply for a job in a different department. She had already done an excellent job for six years in her previous department. She had received nothing but excellent annual reviews and her boss was finally willing to support her transition. So, she got the new job.

Thelma had heard that her new manager, a woman, was known for mistreating other women that reported to her. It was said that she tended to treat the men on her team with a lot more respect.

Thelma was not concerned with this because she had already proven herself in her previous job. Besides, she liked to get to know people for herself.

From the beginning of her new assignment, Thelma saw what everyone was talking about. Her manager began by insulting her during her presentations to the team. When they were both selected for a special company project, the manager let her know that she didn't think Thelma was qualified. She also tried to keep Thelma so busy that she had to struggle to make the special project meetings. Thelma knew that she would not forbid her from participating because the CEO had selected her based on previous work she had done for him.

Thelma decided to go to the manager to speak with her. She wanted to see if there was any way she could make the situation better. She explained that she felt some discrimination toward her. She admitted that she may have misunderstood and wondered if there was something she had done to upset her. The manager flew into a tirade. She told Thelma that none of her employees had ever complained about her management style and that Thelma was obviously the problem.

Things got worse. The manager continued to belittle Thelma in front of her peers. She even started giving subtle insults during the special project meetings. Thelma, frustrated and upset, decided to go to the CEO for assistance. Thelma felt she could trust him. She had had several meetings with him and he was always very friendly.

Thelma told him about the situation and he promised to look into it. Thelma was confident that he would.

The next morning, Thelma's manager stormed into her office and demanded that she go see the Employee Assistance Counselor (EAC). Thelma was shocked and asked why. The manager told her that she was uncoachable and was not a team player. She resented authority and was causing conflict within the group. She also stated that if Thelma didn't straighten up, she would be looking for another job. "Consider yourself on probation. If the EAC does not help you improve within the next few months, you will be out of here." Then, she left. Thelma was in tears. She knew that somehow her manager had found out about her meeting with the executive. Her manager had taken her six years of hard work and loyalty to the company and shoved it right back in her face.

Thelma wiped her tears and went to the EAC office. Three months later, she went to work for a competitor.

* *

The truth is that loyalty in the workplace is blind and unless you have been inducted as a member, you and your concerns require no attention or consideration. Simply stated, as it relates to this situation, you have not earned the right to bring anything to anyone's attention, so fall in line. Do a mediocre job. Sit back and watch people steal from the company. Put up with their discrimination. Ignore any and all problems. Enjoy your paycheck. Go shopping.

* *

WIP #5

We teach by what we do and what we allow.
As a leader, if you want to teach confidence
and trust, you have to Deliver it!
Demonstrate it! Demand it!

ROUND 6

Speaking of Open Doors...

Let me broach this topic with this question, "what brilliant person thought that cubicles would make people more productive in the workplace?" I am of the opinion that this is probably the worst thing that could have happened to it.

Maybe that's a little unfair.

Ok, someone had a good idea that would work in a certain environment, but like every good idea in this world, people began to do it without thinking and it became a "law."

Environments where the work is based on a standard script, for example, data entry, telemarketing, some administrative jobs, etc., can benefit from this type of office arrangement. It's cost effective and provides an efficient way to pack more people into a space. But in jobs such as computer programming, engineering and others that require intense concentration, this setup can be extremely unproductive. Distracting! Achieving the concentration level required in many of these positions is very difficult when your neighbor is having a weekly conference call or an hourly check-in to the suspicious spouse. Not only is it frustrating, but it can also stifle ingenuity and innovation.

The cubicle has turned the workplace into a "Peyton Place" with enough drama for primetime television. More sad than frustrating is the fact that many of our co-workers, aware of the unsuspecting audience now held captive, use this "platform" as an opportunity to get attention. To herald the possibility that there is something interesting in their miserable little lives. These are usually the loud, obnoxious, obtrusive people that have exhausted your list of excuses for declining lunch and shared coffee breaks. They have even exhausted your use of hasty exits from your own cubicle upon their arrival. This being the case, cubicles are obviously not the way to build a cohesive team in the workplace.

I am of the opinion that this lack of privacy is a major contributor to much of the bitterness and hostility among co-workers. If a husband and wife team finds that a little separation makes their relationship more exciting and even bearable, don't you think that a team of strangers cramped together five days a week can benefit from the same. Oh, I guess that's what weekends are for.

Over the years, I have personally learned to ignore conversations around my workspace or to use headphones and play music. But, these situations can become a catch-22. I have often been labeled as unsociable. Which is more important in the workplace, socializing or productivity? Some days it's difficult to tell. And on any day the lack of either could be grounds for termination.

What? I don't have all the answers. Give everybody private offices or build higher, solid walls around the cubicles.

● ●

WIP #6

There is a time and place for everything. The workplace is for work. The time is for working. But things don't have to be so rigid, just limit the time you spend goofing off and learn to use your inside voices.

ROUND 7

Politically Correct Oppression

Much like the invention of the cubicle, words, phrases, and concepts also become cliché. They can even become a kind of dogma. People begin to use them without thinking. As a result, the original intent gets lost. In the workplace, there are many of them. My favorite is the "teamwork" concept.

Growing up in a family of ten has helped me to understand the importance of teamwork. I am not opposed to it. But the workplace is filled with unproductive workers at all levels that use the team concept as a sledgehammer. They use all of their energy to pound this concept into your head so they have none left to put into the actual work.

A really productive worker can't seem to get a break. On one side they have to deal with managers using (abusing) the teamwork concept to suppress their "superstar" ability. On the other side there are lazy co-workers that want to share in the rewards of their hard work but not the actual sweat.

Definition:(Ty's Book of Definitions)
superstar–one that can do and will do many things well.

Another characteristic is he/she enjoys the excitement of work and refuses to be lazy. The sweat required is just as exciting as the reward gained to this person.

Everyone has to pull their weight in order to have a winning team–a strong team. I am of the opinion that originally the team concept had an actual unifying, solidifying impact in the workplace. It encouraged all players to work together and to share information to deliver the best results.

Then, one day...

Lazy, lurking team members (looking for ways to get out of work) began to realize that this concept made allowances for their mediocrity. It allowed them to be rewarded for the work of others, hence, the decline of the true teamwork concept. It has now become extremely oppressive in the workplace. Managers have gotten so used to hearing themselves say it that they forget to think about how they are applying it. At any moment, "you are not a part of the team," can be hurled at you like an unexpected fastball too high and too far left of home plate. Unless you are fast enough to get out of the way, the result is some kind of injury, even if it only hurts for a few seconds.

When managers use the concept improperly, it feels just like a physical beat down. A sucker-punch to the chest from a bully twice your size. A gut-wrenching ache. All of these things are happening to you at once and you are nowhere near friendly territory. The point is that it is unexpected and undeserved. Everything you know about teamwork told you to pull your own weight so that no one else has to, but your manager obviously has a better understanding of the concept. This serves only to increase hostility and resentment among co-workers. Productive employees feel mistreated and overworked and the unproductive, oblivious to any inequity, never improve. The end result is a weak team that is a huge liability rather than an asset.

I learned to anticipate the teamwork speech whenever I expressed my disagreement with a particular solution or whenever I pointed out some blatant weakness in a strategy or worse in our organization. Geesh, good managers are supposed to welcome discriminating eyes and ears. It is their duty to eliminate weaknesses within the company. There are some that would prefer to eliminate the strength. A conscientious, hardworking employee does not intimidate a good leader. A good leader would be able to harness the hard work and set the proper direction so that both the company and the employee would benefit.

While it is a good idea to encourage people to work together, it is not a good idea to suppress or ignore strong individual contributors. Many times they are singly responsible for many successes and should be rewarded. Recognizing individual contributions can encourage healthy competition among team members. It encourages everyone to be better. This is how you build a strong team. I wonder what Michael Jordan would be like right now if Phil Jackson had asked him to hold back a little of his "airness" because he was outshining his teammates. How many championships would the Chicago Bulls have won? It seems ridiculous to suggest this, doesn't it?

＊ ＊ ＊ ＊ ＊ ＊ ＊ ＊ ＊ ＊ ＊ ＊ ＊ ＊ ＊ ＊ ＊ ＊ ＊ ＊

Eric, Phd., was known throughout the company for jumping in on engineering projects at the last minute. He had become so successful at this that he had his name on twelve patents without having made any significant contributions to the work. But at the last minute, he would make some small suggestion, correct a spelling or grammatical error and sign his name. No one ever objected or said anything to him. His manager didn't. His peers didn't. No one. They just continue to talk behind his back and he continues to collect patents.

• •

I am of the opinion that it is up to the managers as well as each employee to ensure that everyone does a fair share of the work and does not waste the company's money. Unfortunately, because workplace confrontations are frowned upon, no one wants to do the confronting, which means there is no assurance. But when done respectfully, confrontations usually yield valuable results.

Most employees see the work habits of co-workers as a private matter, discussed only behind the individuals' backs. This couldn't be further from the truth. The work habits affect the company's profits. The profitability of the company affects every employee.

• •

WIP #7

A chain is only as strong as its weakest link. Find the weakest link and pull it out, or make it as strong as the others.

"Things are really getting hot!"

ROUND 8

The Work Between Breaks

Personally, I prefer to maximize eight hours and get the heck out of the building. Put quite simply, I prefer to have a LIFE. But apparently, this is an obscure concept in the workplace.

The current corporate America standard is as follows:

The workday should begin with a twenty-minute coffee break. An acceptable daily routine would begin with picking up a cup of coffee and heading back to your cubicle. But not before stopping off at the neighbor's cubicle for a recap of yesterday's coffee and cigarette breaks. For efficiency, always take this opportunity to arrange meeting times for the rest of today's breaks. The real pros have figured out how to use this routine and still get paid for a few hours of overtime each day.

My husband likes to talk about the unofficial, undesignated building "**ushers.**" That's what he calls them. These are the smokers and smokers' friends that have to take their breaks outside. They greet you in the morning when you walk in and they are still there to bid you farewell at the end of the day. He says that they never enter the building. I say that they enter to refill their coffee cups or to rush to the bathroom.

The ushers are actually so adept at their routine that the unobservant actually perceives them as "work-aholics." Like they really do work long hard hours. This really takes genius. If you include the amount of mental time they must spend on this deception, the total time spent on actual work would average less than an hour each day.

This practice has become quite common in small startup companies. Since there is much more work per person in these smaller companies, you are automatically expected to be in the building long hours–from sunrise to sunset. So everyone tries to live up to this image. But it's just a façade because no one's working. Apparently, it doesn't matter what you do during the workday, as long as you are in the building.

What makes it worse is that most of these companies provide breakfast and dinner, so it isn't really difficult to persuade people to stay. However, this does make it more difficult to get them to work. At one company, people played ping-pong for a few hours in the middle of the day and ended up working until as late as nine or ten in the evening.

Please, don't misunderstand what I'm saying. I see absolutely nothing wrong with this if it is acceptable with management and the work gets done. What I have a problem with is this becoming the standard.

People that actually come in on time, work eight hours (avoiding the caffeine and nicotine breaks) and go home to their families, find themselves among the outcasts. The perception seems to be that they are not as diligent as those that work the late hours. What is even more fatal is the perception that the work they do is obviously not challenging enough since they get it done in only eight hours. And they thought it was because they were efficient. Intelligent. Focused. Such arrogance is unacceptable!

WIP #8

While you are making your list of things not to steal from the company, place TIME at the top. Time is most valuable because you can't give it back or replace it.

ROUND 9

Join the Frequent Flyers

I enjoy talking about these professionals. These are the people that have mastered company sponsored road trips. The trips are commonly disguised as important customer meetings. The entire strategy or deception is built upon increasing the frequent flyer miles. *Can you say family vacation?* This is indisputably among the list of ideal perks for any job. I mean, *careeeeeer!*

The frequent flyers are usually the guys that are never in the office when they should be. I am not referring to field personnel whose very title indicates that they are most likely not in the office. They are required to travel and besides that, they usually document such travel with detailed field reports. No, I am referring to others in positions that allow them to travel if and when they deem it necessary. For example, anyone in the Marketing, Sales or Customer Service organization, would not be above suspicion. I would be included in this category.

I once worked closely with a sales executive that liked to brag about all of his frequent flyer points and how his entire family flew to Hawaii without paying one dime. This can be a great incentive when your career requires that you travel a lot. But your road trips should produce some revenue for the company. In this case, it did not. And to my surprise, this was never a problem among the good ole' boys, the other executives. They didn't seem to care that he was flying all over the country spending more money than he was bringing in. They liked him. He was one of them.

One of my most favorite co-workers, Bill, a sales veteran of 25 years, was an avid golfer. Most of his customer meetings took place on the golf course. But Bill was different in his approach. He admitted that he wanted to play golf, but he made sure that he walked off the course with a purchase order or a promise for one. I have a lot of respect for him. He did his job.

Have you ever noticed how a customer meeting becomes critical whenever the customer is located near a four star resort or a great golf course?

Bill realized that no matter where he held his customer meetings, the company would have to pay for it. Therefore, he chose places that would add more excitement to the work, but he kept the company business as his priority. There is nothing wrong with finding ways to make your work exciting. But when the excitement becomes the priority on company time, which means company money, there is an integrity issue.

Ahhh! What's the point? I don't want to rain on anyone's parade, so...if you set your sights on staying in corporate America, join the frequent flyers. I am of the opinion that frequent flyers are envied and considered paragons of professionalism.

• •

WIP #9

Privileges extended by the company are given as a convenience. It is expected that the conveniences will yield assets for the company. But when you abuse them, they only produce liabilities and you, the abuser, are the biggest liability of all.

ROUND 10

How To Make An Emotional Decision

I am probably going to have the most fun writing this round because it will allow me to unveil a gross misconception that has been used to oppress many professional women.

Let me begin by saying, if you are a human being, you make emotional decisions every day. Women do and yes, men do also. If you are living, breathing, thinking and feeling, you are guaranteed to make an emotional decision *TODAY! Right now!*

It is a fact that women tend to be more open and honest with their feelings. We are even more passionate at times. But we are no more prone to emotional decisions than men. Unless you consider us to be more human.

One of my previous managers had so fallen for this "women make emotional decisions" crap that she had turned herself into a cold heartless... She walked around desperately trying to avoid smiles and friendly greetings. She thought that as long as she appeared tough, she wasn't emotional and no one would think that she was incapable of being in total control. Many times she appeared to be so in control that she was like a robot. It was ridiculous. I knew it. Everyone knew it.

One day while everyone gathered in the auditorium for an assembly, I watched this manager deliberately walk past a young woman and bump her with her shoulder. I saw her purposely scurry through a group of nearby people to get close enough to do it. She hit her so hard that she almost knocked her over. This young woman had previously sent her a memo outlining major problems with the special project she was managing. I knew that she could be pretty nasty but she usually demonstrated it with more subtlety. This just seemed so...juvenile. The young woman didn't have the rank to complain. Furthermore, she probably thought it was just an accident. I knew it wasn't because I had watched the manager set herself up for it. She didn't even excuse herself. She just kept walking. I say that was an emotional decision, don't you?

Oh, by the way, this manager was one of the speakers at the assembly. Her topic was on increasing company moral.

* *

Bob didn't receive his deserved and expected promotion today. His manager had practically guaranteed that he would. Apparently, he changed his mind.

The reason cited was that Bob had a problem with teamwork. His manager went on to say that a few of Bob's co-workers made a few comments about his lack of cooperation at times. Since they were brought to his attention, he felt it best that he allow Bob the opportunity to improve before promoting him. Bob was promised another opportunity if the improvement took place before the next review period.

Quite understandably, Bob was shocked when he received the news. He was heart broken and confused. He could not accept the answer his manager gave him. He wanted to know what went wrong because just twenty-four hours earlier, he was assured that he was on his way up in the company. The CEO, in an effort to get to know him, had even invited him to play a game of golf at his country club. Bob was sure that he had really impressed him. He played his best game and won!

* *

Susan always worked well with John. He respected her ideas and counted on her opinion. They often traveled together on customer visits and other company business. Although John was her boss, he treated her as an equal not a subordinate. Their relationship while close, was strictly professional. The CEO often said that they were an excellent team.

Then John's wife met Susan for the first time at the office Christmas party. The next week, a budget problem caused Susan's position to be eliminated immediately. She was offered another job within the company in another state. Surprised and backed into a corner, she accepted.

Just for kicks, I will give a description of Susan. She is approximately 5'5", 125 lbs with long, naturally blonde hair. A gentleman once stopped her in the Atlanta airport and asked her for an autograph. He thought she was Kim Bassinger.

* *

James was quoted in a telecommunications magazine after giving a great presentation at a trade show. The entire industry caught a buzz from what he said and began to quote him in other articles. He received a lot of publicity. It was very exciting.

James' job is marketing manager so he is the one that works with the PR (Public Relations) agencies and other public representation of his company. He is very good at his job and has a great understanding of telecommunications, the technology and the industry. He is always well dressed and receives a lot of attention. As a result of James' popularity, a local business program called him to be a panelist on their show. James reported directly to the CEO so before he accepted, he went to find out if he would approve.

The CEO told James that he should not make any public appearances on behalf of the company anymore. This confused James because public appearances were a major part of his job. The CEO took James' place on the show. He embarrassed the company because his knowledge of the industry was not as detailed as James' and he had little experience.

Later James found out from one of the administrators that the CEO had expressed great disapproval of the publicity that James was getting. The CEO's Executive Assistant that revealed this information quoted the CEO as saying: "I am the front man in this company; everyone needs to understand that."

James was very hurt by this. He had suspected that the CEO was a bit jealous but James always supported his boss and would never intentionally "overstep" him.

* *

These are probably just strange coincidences.

However, if you are honest about human nature, you will probably make the same conclusions that I did. Envy, jealousy, resentment, insecurity, bruised egos, massive egos, pain, anger, happy households, unhappy households–all are many times a major factor in decision making for each of us. Those of us that consider ourselves decent human beings, while making our emotional decisions, usually try to avoid destroying lives in the process.

Moral: Get over yourself! Everyone makes emotional decisions.

● ● ● ● ● ● ● ● ● ● ● ● ● ● ● ● ● ● ●

WIP #10

As human beings, our emotions will play a part in the decisions we make. A mature decision, one that demonstrates control of those emotions, will yield a win-win solution or at least fewer casualties.

ROUND 11

The Middleman

I started calling my manager the middleman for several reasons. I saw him as an unnecessary and expensive step on my success ladder–a step I wanted to eliminate. A big boulder from down under that somehow rolled smack dab into the middle of my road to happiness. More specifically, the name indicated how I felt about the unnecessarily high price I paid for everything I achieved. And finally, I always seemed to get along great with his bosses but never with him. I could accomplish much more when I circumvented him and went straight to the top. He was arrogant, selfish and clueless. Therefore, he was for me a middleman.

All managers should NOT be considered middlemen. When there is a great relationship with a manager, it is very easy to accept and understand their coaching. Their leadership is a necessary part of your effectiveness and your professional growth. The middleman manager that I am referring to is the manager that never has any ideas of his own. He only seems to come alive when he can add fifty million revisions to your ideas. Sometimes (rarely) they may be needed, but most of the time, this is just his way of reminding you that he has the final say in everything. He immediately recognizes that you are not intimidated. Oops. His most effective tool in his leadership toolbox isn't working. He feels that you disregard him. Oops. There goes another broken tool because he craves the attention of his subordinates. You don't compliment him or suck-up. Yikes! He has nothing left to manage you with. You are therefore unmanageable.

This middleman is not interested in helping you establish a career but rather in reminding you that this is just a job and you are just a workhorse. This is always disheartening for a conscientious employee. The primary goal is always to please the manager. Make his or her job easier. Make them look good. Make them never regret that you were hired. The goal is to receive their rewards and their encouragement.

The middleman will always forget that there is great dignity in doing good work and getting the compliments and the rewards from the manager for a job well done. The middleman mistakenly identifies the "gung-ho" attitude of the newcomer as trying to be better than everyone else. Instead, it is more about trying to be as good as everyone else. Personally, the only time I even considered that maybe my work was better than some others was after being asked (several times) "Do you think you are better than everyone else?" No, I don't but obviously you do. Thanks!

Middleman managers have been hiding behind their "badges" for too long. When someone comes along that does not need their micro-managing and can function independently, they discover the holes in their leadership abilities. They can't seem to think of anything to do if they can't lord over you and micro-manage your entire workday. One would think that they would welcome your independence since it would give them the freedom to do other things. A-ha! Maybe that's the problem.

Middleman managers can only oversee the execution of simple tasks passed down from upper management. They prefer to hide behind getting these things done so that they appear to be good managers. But, if there is a need for new ideas or concepts to sustain or reposition the company in a volatile market, they have no clues. NONE!

* *

I once worked for a manager that actually had one of my co-workers spy on me. I noticed it because whenever I would pass him in the hallway, about 15 minutes later, I would get an email from my manager with a long list of trivial crap that needed to get done right away. I tested it a few times before I drew this ridiculous conclusion. It was true. He was determined to manage every millisecond of my time.

I found out later, from another young woman that had once worked for him, that his problem went well beyond micromanaging. It was more about stereotypes. Women obviously needed more attention from him no matter how well they did their jobs. When I accepted the position in his department, it was one of two that were offered to me. He seemed very laid back and friendly so I chose his group. I didn't know that he had a problem with women–independent women. I did notice, however, that I was the only female in my group. But that didn't raise any flags because many times that was the case in very technical environments.

After the "heads-up" from this young woman and a few more inquiries, I found out that he was definitely thought of as a male chauvinist. Well, needless to say, I had to figure out how to work around him. I couldn't. He was constantly on my case. He wanted weekly meetings. Detailed progress reports. Drafts of everything, which he constantly revised so that they would never be complete. He was exhausting.

Because he rarely allowed me to finish anything, I never reached many of those small milestones, short-term accomplishments, and my confidence was slowly deteriorating.

Finally, I decided to speak with him about it. He insisted that I was mistaken. He thought that I did really good work. None of the guys were working on projects that required his constant oversight. That's why they didn't have weekly meetings with him. No one was spying on me. It was mere coincidence with the emails. He didn't convince me, but I dropped it. I concluded that he had absolutely nothing to do and he just didn't want me to know it. But he only succeeded in heralding that point. I didn't want to make it personal. I was very young and naïve then.

Eventually, after a few more of the email scenarios, I started to ignore them. When he inquired, I would remind him of the important projects I was already in the middle of. All of the guys seemed to escape with the "full plate" excuse, so I decided to try it. A few other times I reminded him that he had an administrative support person that could perform most of the tasks he was requesting from me. I think I surprised him to the point of shock. He stopped sending the "spy mails" and I could finally go to the restroom without penalty.

* * * * * * * * * * * * * * * * * * *

Working in the corporate environment has helped me to understand that no matter how much authority a person has, if he or she has any insecurities in any areas, everyone presents a threat, even those with no authority.

With all that I have learned in the workplace, there is still one thing that baffles me:

"Why is MY manager always the biggest idiot in the company?"

● ●

WIP #11

As a manager, you are expected to teach and to direct. Your effectiveness depends on knowing when and how much of each is required.

ROUND 12

Now Entering Gang Territory

I prefer the multi-colored bandannas, physical threats, verbal threats and profanity. At least then I would know that I was entering a hostile environment, a possible gang territory. The physical threat of injury from something like a drive-by shooting would induce less anxiety than some of the emotional pain inflicted by groups of hostile people in the workplace. I call them "corporate gangs."

Definition: (from Webster)
gang–a group of criminals or hoodlums who band together for mutual protection and profit; to harass or attack as a group

"Corporate gangs" or "workplace gangs" are the groups of co-workers whose sole modus operandi, M.O. or mode of operation, is to beat down other co-workers should they oppose any of the gang's great ideas or get too much attention. They resort to harassment, disparagement, isolation, and any other obvious and convenient form of distress available.

Most common in every company are: The Coffee Gang, The Water Cooler Gang, The Cigarette Gang, and The Lunch Gang. These are all forms of corporate gangs whose names indicate from where they launch their attacks. They all have the same basic M.O. and are distinguished only by where and how they meet. Because of their names, they are often mistaken for "cliques," but to be a clique would require a change in the

M.O., or rather the lack of one.

Definition: (from Webster)
clique–an exclusive group of friends or associates

• •

Monica usually supported the team-building outings. She was the one that originally started the day trips for the marketing group. But, this time the group wanted to go away for an entire weekend to a resort out of state and Monica was strongly opposing it. She had two young children and did not want to leave them for three days. Not for something like this. Since she was in charge of planning these events, the director allowed her to make the final decision. She compromised and chose a one-night stay at a closer resort within driving distance. So, everyone would still have two full days together, Thursday and Friday, rather than the weekend.

Coming out of the meeting, Monica knew that the group was disappointed, but they had worked closely together for so long that she knew they would get beyond this. Certainly, they would not resent her for it. Besides, she did compromise.

For the next week, Monica noticed that she wasn't getting email notifications of scheduled meetings. She wouldn't find out until the last minute and as a result, she was late a few times. Monica hated being late. She also noticed that no one seemed to have time to go to lunch with her. Even worse, those that went to lunch found excuses not to bring anything back for her when she couldn't go. No one from her group stopped by her cubicle in the morning or in the afternoon. She knew that everyone was giving her the cold shoulder and she didn't like it.

Monica went home that weekend and talked with her husband about the weekend team-building event. She planned with him to have his mother come take the kids to her place for that particular weekend. She didn't tell him how she was being treated because he would have encouraged her not to succumb to their hostility. But Monica didn't like conflict. She was used to everyone liking her.

During the Monday morning meeting, she told everyone that her in-laws wanted to take the kids for a weekend. She said she was hoping that no one would mind if she planned the weekend trip instead of what was previously decided. She also said she hoped it didn't present any inconveniences for anyone. No one opposed the change. They all agreed to plan the weekend activities over the lunch hour.

● ●

The cold harsh reality is that these gangs are no different from street gangs. One might go further and say that street gangs show more integrity. They are honest about their intent. You know you are going to get a beat down. But these corporate gangs disguise themselves in expensive suits. You assume they're not dangerous. Bring it on! You've sized them up and you can handle it if it gets physical. And then like snakes, they launch their sneak attack. When you least expect it! When you are most vulnerable! You are not prepared! What happened to the fair fights, the physical stuff?!

Once again, I have surprised you with my terminology. Forget the corporate dream for a moment and think about it. The location of the clubhouse doesn't change the M.O. Here, the gang members meet in corporate offices. But, they still attack without reason. They bond over territory. They exclude due to prejudice. They have no remorse for their actions. Where I come from, we call that a gang. What do you call it?

Remember my manager from Round 10: How To Make An Emotional Decision? She launched a physical assault on a young woman just for doing her job. Well, it would have been fine had it not revealed that the manager had done a poor job. No one ever suspected that this manager would try to beat down another woman in the workplace.

* *

WIP #12

An organized group with a great idea can invoke positive and necessary changes in the workplace. The goal is the more productive workplace, not THE GROUP.

"Are you angry with me yet?"

ROUND 13

Virtual Qualifications

My friends love to discuss this topic. They all have many examples that support the point that I make here.

Let me begin by giving you a definition for "virtual" from Webster's dictionary.

Definition:
virtual–existing in effect or essence though not in actual fact, form or name.

In many of my jobs, I have met people that thought they could do my job as well as I or better. Although I always considered it to be a very bold posture, I was never really offended. My idea of what I contributed to all of my workplaces was one that encompassed everything about me. The work I produced was only a portion of that contribution.

The fact is that every reasonable professional acknowledges the possibility of someone else in the same profession doing a better job. This being the case, I always looked forward to at least one of *THESE* boasters presenting evidence to support their position. But, since that would actually require doing work, it never happened. This is why I call them "virtual qualifications." They exist only in essence, no fact or form, and the essence is only in their minds. *I* produced the work. *I* was qualified. *I* had the credentials. These are the things they wanted to challenge. Not because they wanted to do my job, but they resented the fact that *I* could do my job and quite well.

To support their case, I must say that many times the end result of much hard work appears to be simple and easy. However, the end result does not always depict the full scope of the work. Depending on the subject, it could take years of study and research to be able to dissect and present information that even a child can understand.

This is another point not understood by those with only virtual qualifications because it requires actual study, not the essence of study. It requires actual work, not the essence of work. And sometimes most importantly, it requires an actual piece of paper (a college degree) that proves you actually learned during the study and the work, not just the essence of that piece of paper.

* *

My friend Paul is a lawyer. One of his clients, Ernie, was arrested for driving under the influence. Apparently, Ernie had just left a birthday party and usually does not drink but decided to have one glass of champagne.

There was a random police check nearby so when Ernie left the party, he was stopped and subsequently arrested. Although he only had one drink, because he wasn't used to drinking, he was a bit "influenced."

They went to court and with what appeared to be very little effort, Paul got the charges dropped and Ernie went home happy and relieved. However, he paid quite a handsome fee for what appeared to be very little effort from Paul. He called Paul to complain and told him that he could have done the same job and kept his money. Paul encouraged him to do that next time because he was not getting his money back.

A year later Ernie went to court after being involved in another car accident. This time, the other driver was under the influence of alcohol and was also speeding. There was some discrepancy about whether Ernie had actually stopped at a stop sign or possibly caused the accident himself. Since there were no other witnesses, they were both given traffic citations.

Ernie paid his citation and assumed it was all over. However, he received a letter stating that the drunk driver was suing him. Ernie decided that this was obviously a ridiculous case and any judge or jury would see right through his opponent. So, he felt that he could represent himself after seeing the effortless way Paul had represented him previously. Besides, this time he was totally innocent.

By the time the case was over, Ernie had to pay the medical bills of the drunk driver and more. The jury didn't seem to care about the DUI citation the drunk driver had received. His defense was that he was right around the corner from his house and would have never endangered anyone if Ernie had not run the stop sign. The interesting and convincing (to this particular jury) part of the testimony from the drunk driver was the reason he was even in his car when Ernie hit him.

His story was that he had a couple of drinks after a heated argument with his wife. He really doesn't like arguing with his wife so he always feels really bad. They made up after the fight and she mentioned that she needed some gas in her car. He never lets his wife get her own gas, so he went out to fill her tank so she wouldn't have to stop the following morning. On his way home, Ernie ran into him.

Well, all seven of the women on the jury understood exactly why Ernie was the guilty party.

What Ernie failed to realize is that Paul studied law for four years. Paul has a law degree. Paul's years of experience is what gives him the ability to make his work appear effortless. That experience is what Ernie was paying for. An inexperienced lawyer may have demonstrated more sweat, but that doesn't win cases. It takes skill and practice, both of which Paul demonstrates very well.

Paul would have gotten more information about Ernie's case before going to court. He would not have gone in unprepared or with only the preparation of "I am innocent. The other guy was drunk." He would have found out that this drunk driver was in his wife's car because his was being repaired. He knocked out the right headlight when he ran into the garage the week before. By the way, he was drunk then also. Paul learned these few details from someone that knew someone that knew the drunk driver and had heard him telling his "funny story" over a few drinks the following week. Paul didn't think it was funny. He felt bad for Ernie, but I thought it was hilarious.

* * * * * * * * * * * * * * * * * * * *

People like Ernie have to learn the hard way. I recall a marketing meeting in which Donna, the Marketing Administrator, boldly declared, with the support of my manager, that she would be willing to move into my current position so that I could take on a different project. While I appreciated the gesture, I was surprised that she thought she could do my job. According to office gossip, she gained this confidence while sharing pillow talk with my manager. Apparently her virtual qualifications became more blatant during these moments of...closeness.

The ironic part of this particular situation is that much of what she saw me doing was already her job. She had obviously been in a position to refuse to do her duties without consequences and she chose to exercise this privilege regularly. Therefore, I found that it was much easier and faster for me to do many things myself. Those duties that were within the scope of my job description, she rarely saw because they were of no interest to her.

As in the case with Ernie, Donna didn't realize that the years I spent studying in college, in addition to the years of practical experience, gave me the ability to make my work appear effortless. I am not saying that at times their points are not justified. What I am saying is that to assume this bold posture, with only virtual qualifications, is quite risky. Ask Ernie.

My hypocrisy on this subject becomes evident with each visit to my doctor. He spends five minutes with me and I end up with a bill for $250. This is when I boldly declare my virtual qualifications as a physician with statements such as, "Is that all? I could have figured that out myself...blah blah blah."

Oh, and you have never done this, right?

Another supporting argument on behalf of Ernie, Donna and others with only virtual qualifications, is that many times it can be quite disheartening to physically work hard all day, earn very little and then see others do less physical work and earn much more. I guess this could also be an argument in support of higher education. Without it, achieving those simplified outputs that they observed could have been much more difficult and time consuming. Also, the final product may have been less appealing.

Ok, no more nice guy. Here it is...

Your virtual qualifications are just that–virtual! If you sincerely believe that you could produce the same results, I encourage you to begin with making the virtual a reality by getting A CLUE! Until then, do you mind if I just ignore you?

NO OFFENSE!

⊛ ⊛

WIP #13

Experience is not always your best teacher, but the most suitable substitute is usually someone else that has it.

"Oops! That did it!"

ROUND 14

The Mutual Adversary Merger

Similar to the M.O. of the corporate gangs is the intent of what I call the mutual adversary merger–two people that had absolutely nothing in common until both of them discovered their mutual dislike for another co-worker–you. Now, they are the closest team in the workplace, with you as the common enemy. What's ridiculous is that the goals of the company were not enough to bring these people together. It took something bigger. It took you! You gave them this shared hatred. *See, you did add value to your workplace.*

Yes, that will do just fine!

• •

Carol accepted a job as the Sr. Product Marketing Manager for a startup company. In her new position she made herself available to many of her marketing co-workers to assist with any and all projects. She felt this would help her gain a sense of how the department worked as well as gain some credibility with this new team.

Everyone was very happy to request her assistance. They all felt they were overworked and could use the help. She really impressed everyone with her details, timeliness and most of all with the way she stuck to her schedule. If she promised it by Wednesday, it was done by Wednesday. All of her co-workers commended her on her teamwork. Soon everyone in the company knew her to be reliable and began requesting her help as well as recommending her for high profile projects.

Susan, the Marketing Communications Manager, was constantly complaining about her many projects. She was especially happy for the way that Carol had taken on some of her work. She began to confide in Carol about the lack of teamwork from others, especially David. He was responsible for Business Development. Susan went on to say that David really did sloppy work and that she tried to work with him but he just did not care about what he was "putting out." She would rather work around him. Carol was very uncomfortable with this because she had a policy of taking her problems directly to the source and did not believe in talking about people behind their backs. She found that people respected her for that, once they got over the initial shock of the confrontation.

Carol suggested to Susan that she speak with David and try to help him improve in the areas where she thought he was lacking. It would be best for everyone if she did. Susan stated that he was very sensitive and she had tried talking to him about it but he did not accept constructive criticism very well. She preferred to stay away from him. "I just do my job and let him do his" was her final statement on the issue. Carol didn't mention it again.

One day David, having completed a technical document, sent it around to the marketing team for their input and suggestions. Everyone responded immediately that it was "great," "wonderful," "lot of good work," etc. Carol, on the other hand, read it very carefully. This was information that would be given to potential customers about her product so she wanted to make sure it was accurate. It was not.

Carol saw that many of the specifications David listed were very old. He mentioned features that were not on the product roadmap and left out features that were. He also left out the key differentiators that had really gotten the attention of the industry. The document could prove to be destructive to the goals of the company. She decided to send David an email and request a meeting with him. After hearing about how sensitive he was, she wanted to speak with him directly and not risk the misunderstanding that could result from making the corrections through email.

Carol pointed out the problems with the document as well as the good points. She made a few suggestions and gave David the latest specifications and roadmaps on the product. She also gave him a presentation she had just completed which high-lighted the key differentiators of the product. She could sense that he was not happy about her corrections but he did not say anything.

The next morning, as Carol approached the building, she noticed Susan and David talking outside. She thought that it was good for them to be talking since Susan had mentioned that she could not talk to him and tries to stay away from him. When Carol greeted them, neither of them returned the greeting. This disturbed her.

Later that morning, Carol passed them again. This time near the restrooms. They were leaning on the wall and appeared to be very angry about something. She stopped and asked if everything was ok and was told that the matter did not concern her. She walked away confused and a little hurt.

Immediately after lunch, Mark, the Director of Marketing, called Carol into his office. He told her that David and Susan had spoken to him about the way she had been criticizing their work. He told her that she was to do her job and leave the managing to him. Carol was very confused and choked up. She felt as if she had been hit in the gut with a boulder. She managed to explain to him what had happened with David. However, she was totally lost with the Susan issue. She had no idea that there was a problem with her. She was under the impression that they had formed a friendship.

As time passed and Carol got to know everyone, she realized that Susan resented her for being able to do her job as well as assist others. She also realized that she resented her versatility and sudden popularity. Most of all, she resented the way everyone had started to request Carol's help and then rave about her responsiveness.

Eventually, Carol realized that what brought Susan and David together was their mutual dislike for her. Then again, not really her as a person but the threat they felt because of her abilities. In the blink of an eye, they had something in common and a mutual adversary to talk about.

* * * * * * * * * * * * * * * * * * * *

Most normal people form normal friendships based on similar hobbies or because someone is very interesting and exciting. But adversary mergers are definitely not normal and I find them disgusting. If the only thing that you have in common with this new "best friend" is the dirt you dish on a co-worker, you are desperate and a sad excuse for a human being. I will boldly say that if this is the way you are accustomed to behaving, whatever you think this "mutual adversary" did to you was likely the result of something you initiated.

I have seen these glass mergers over and over again in the workplace. They are not friendships. They are not even the beginnings of friendships. They are fragile disasters waiting to crack up. The only thing that could possibly come out of them is yet another corporate gang.

* *

WIP #14

A confidant at work can be a valuable ally.
Use the time you spend together building
each other up, not tearing others down.

KNOCKDOWN

Observations From the Ground

Ok. It looks like I'm the one that got knocked down. But...I was...robbed...double-teamed! Despite all of that, I gave it a good fight. However, I do realize from down here, in my haze, that this entire process would have been a lot less painful had I used a basketball analogy. Hmmm, yes, I believe that would have spared me quite a bit of...swelling.

Let's see, it may have gone something like this...

By now you may have figured out that I was not actually a player in this volatile game. Maybe I should say that I was not a starter. If I must self-proclaim, in my defense I say, unlike other bench-warmers, it had absolutely nothing to do with my ability. Neither can it be attributed to my zealousness. I was always quite enthusiastic about my particular roles.

Although the starting line-up is a group of good players, there are other good players that are not in the starting line-up. There is much to be said for the support required from the other members of a team. That being said, I am in no way implying that because I didn't start, the game wasn't fair. However, I am pointing out that I did have the ability. But who wants to play in a game without rules? It's just too confusing and frustrating.

I am of the opinion that had I been given a "Phil Jackson-like" coach, a rulebook, rose-colored glasses or a blindfold at birth, and a muzzle, my great talents would have been recognized, displayed, and harnessed. Even the best players need good leadership.

I could not be considered objective if I didn't add that I did have a huge problem. Despite the number of times I observed the way things were done, I continued to expect and demand that they be different. I persisted in pointing out what needed to be changed. Everyone else seemed to go with the flow and disregard the lack of order. As long as there were no confrontations, they were satisfied. Oh well, I guess a more intuitive player would have recognized that those confusing, simple things were indeed the rules: ignore the obvious, assess the vague, and avoid being a part of the problem.

...Yes, that analogy worked quite well. Wow, this would have been a really short book. Anyway, knocked down isn't knocked out, so I have no regrets. I learned a lot. Besides, I still seem to be thinking clearly.

* * * * * * * * * * * * * * * * * * * *

WIP #15

When searching for necessary changes, don't forget to search within yourself. Not only is it the easiest place to start, it is often the place where it is most needed.

Fight's Over!

Thank you for reading!

INTEGRITY

Every MAN must live as a LEADER
There is always someone following.

Every LEADER must live as a JUDGE
He will be asked to decide on matters of those
who follow.

Every JUDGE must live as a DISCIPLE
He must be disciplined to follow a standard.

The STANDARD must be God's Word
For the whole purpose of MAN'S Life
As a LEADER
A JUDGE
A DISCIPLE
Is to love GOD and follow His STANDARD.

– This is dedicated to hardworking
professionals everywhere –

by Ty Brown

About the Author...

Ty Brown was born in Charleston, South Carolina, the ninth child of ten. She entered corporate America after earning both a Bachelors and a Masters degree in Electrical Engineering.

After moving to Silicon Valley for the dot com "gold rush" and finding no gold, she decided to follow her real dream and write her first book. How apropos that it deals with the frustrations of corporate America. "Let's Just Take This Outside!" reveals that even after her disappointment, she is not without a sense of humor.

Working independently, she now consults on "Workplace Improvement Principles," Marketing, and "Principles For Good Customer Service."

Ty lives with her husband in the Northern California-Bay Area.

Quick Order Form

Please send me _____ copies of *"Let's Just Take This Outside!"*

Name:_____

Address:_____

City_____

State_____ Zip_____-_____

Telephone:_____

Email:_____

_____copies x $15.95/copy.

Sales tax:
Please add 8.25% for orders shipped to California.

Shipping: Add $3.25 for the first book; $1.00 for each additional book.

Mail check or money order to:

Katsir Publishing
39720 Paseo Padre Parkway #256
Fremont, CA 94538-1616

See www.katsirpublishing.com for information.